Jesus on a Donkey

KEVIN MAYHEW LTD
Rattlesden Bury St Edmunds
Suffolk England
IP30 0SZ

ISBN 0 86209 499 2

Printed in Great Britain

Jesus on a Donkey

Retold from Scripture by Susan Sayers
and illustrated by Arthur Baker

Kevin Mayhew

Nathan lived on a hill in a village called Bethany.

He had a baby sister called Martha, who sometimes walked, but mostly crawled.

Nathan's family lived at one end of the village, where there were lots of olive and almond trees just right for climbing.

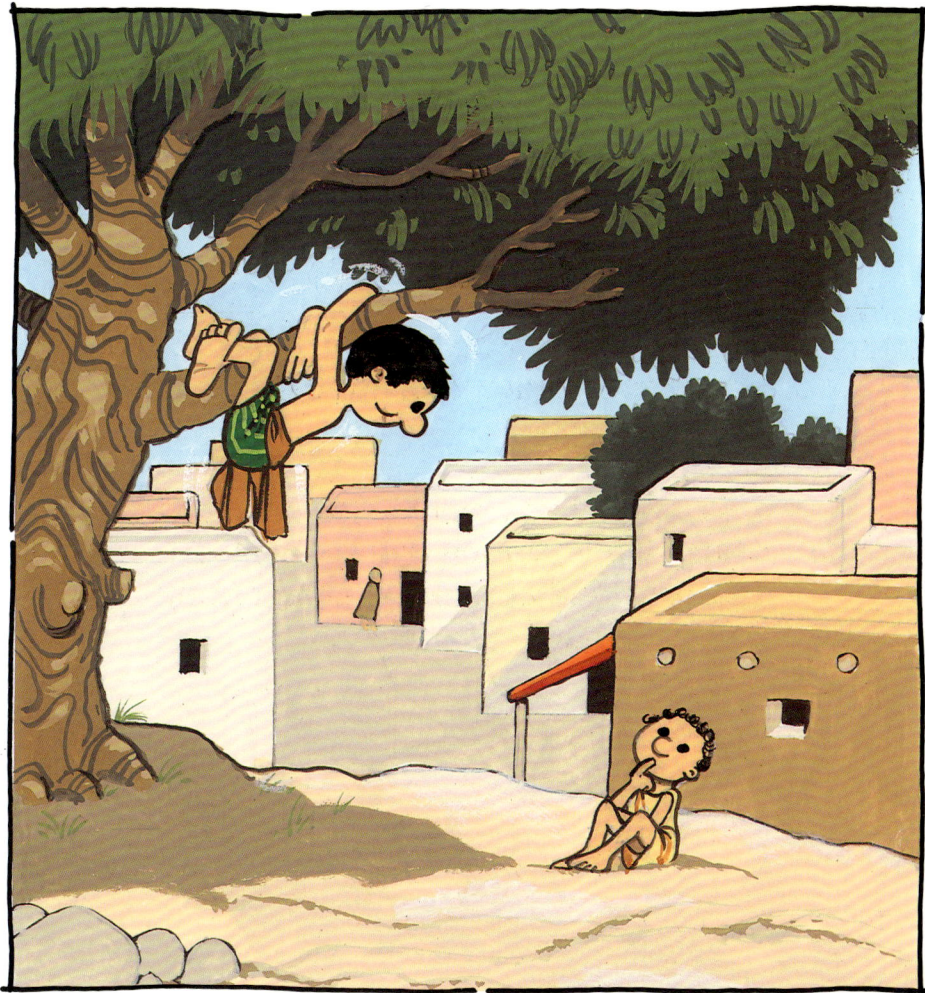

Each year Nathan's father sold the dark, bitter olives and smooth almonds in the Jerusalem market. Nathan helped him gather the fruits and pack them on to the sides of their donkey, Tabitha.

Then Nathan would walk one side of Tabitha, and his father the other, with Tabitha's ears twitching at flies between them.

When Tabitha wasn't needed for carrying, the children sometimes rode on her bristly, grey back.

Little Martha was in front clutching a tuft of grey mane, and Nathan sat behind to hold her on.

Martha squealed and chuckled as Tabitha swayed along nodding at every step.

And going downhill they would slither down her back, nearer and nearer to her tall, soft ears.

It was great fun!

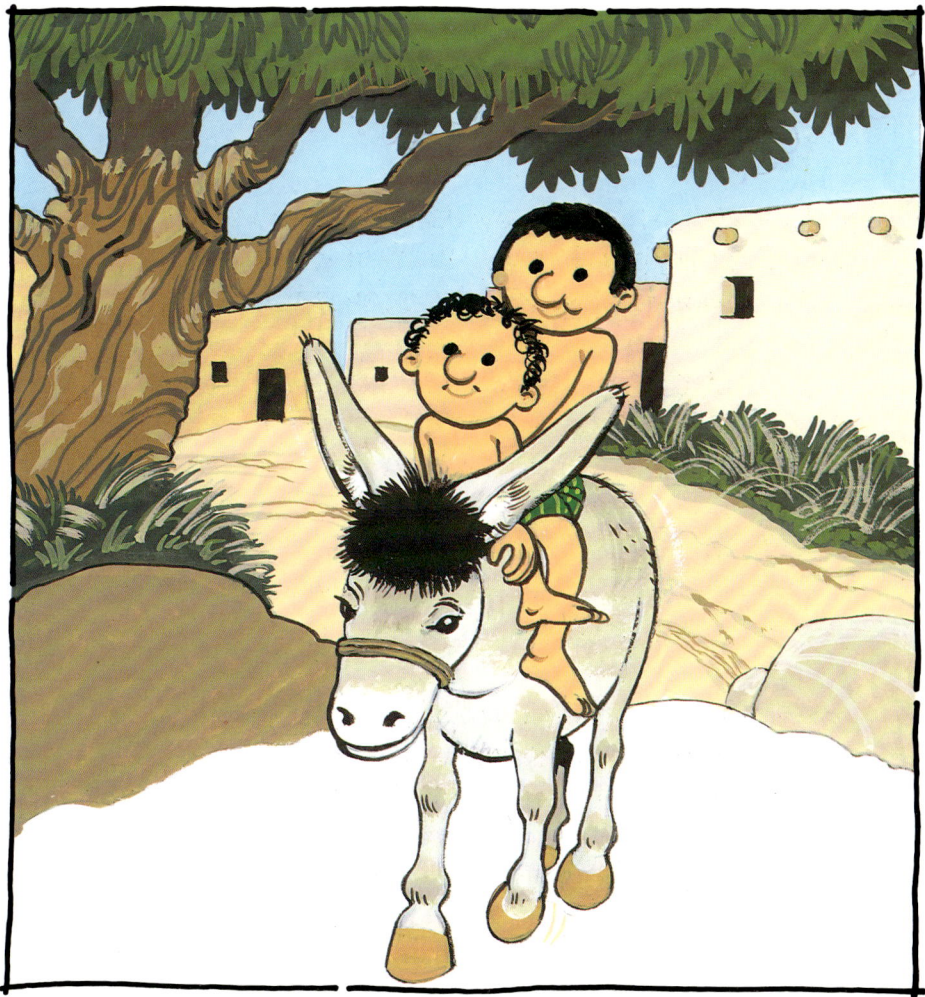

The children loved Tabitha and gave her apples and handfuls of grass to eat, or even a juicy carrot if one could be spared.

And that Spring, Tabitha had given them the sweetest, softest baby donkey!

He had thin, wobbly legs and a fluffed-up grey coat.

They called him Kidron, after the little stony brook in the valley.

And each week Kidron grew stronger and bigger.

One morning Nathan's father
groomed Kidron and then led him
outside.

He tied his halter to the ring in the
stone wall by their doorway.

'Why are you putting Kidron there,
Dad?' asked Nathan.

'Well, son, a special friend needs to
use Kidron today,' he answered
mysteriously, 'and Kidron,'
he went on, smiling, 'is ready and
waiting.'

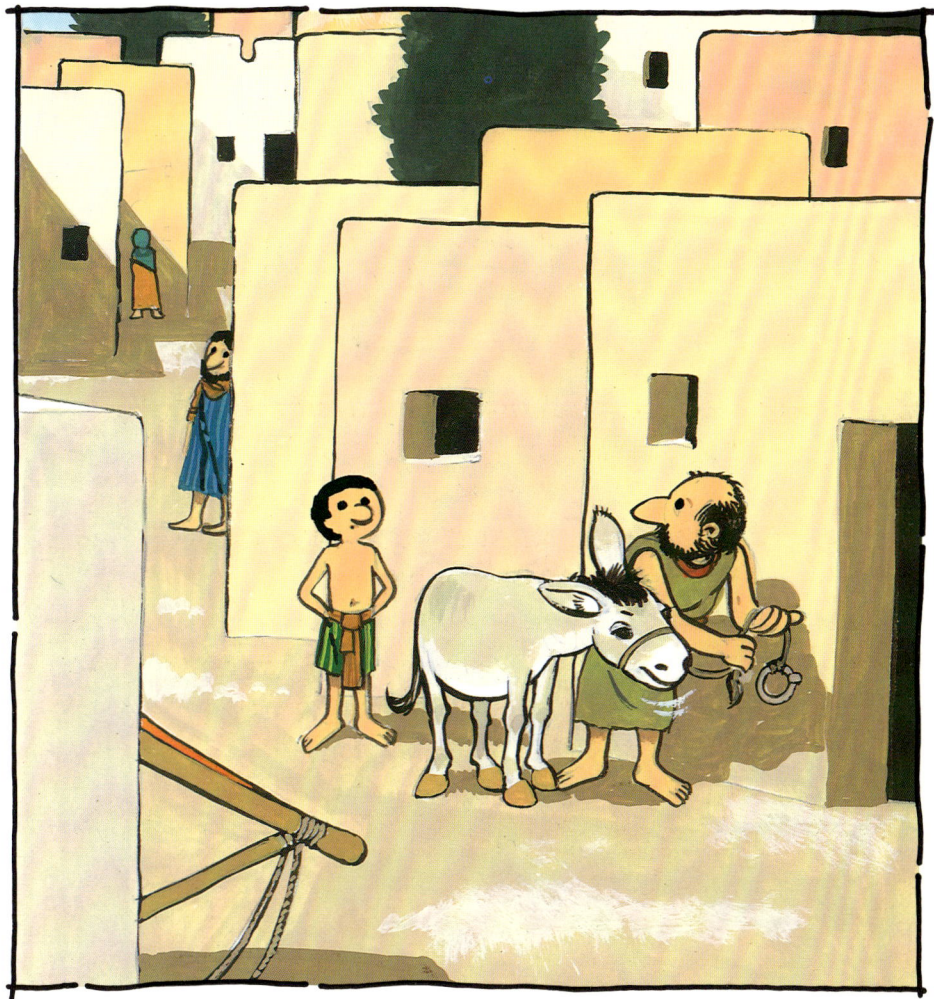

By midday Bethany had become
quite a busy little village.

It was nearly time for the great
Passover Festival, and all morning
groups of people had been
heading for Jerusalem, chattering
or singing as they went.

Nathan watched them as the dust
swirled and the donkeys called
in their harsh, gravelly voices.

Just then he noticed two men leave the main track and come running up the narrow street which led to his house.

They were breathing hard – it was quite a climb.

Kidron was still standing outside the house, flicking his ears lazily.

Nathan watched the two men stop when they reached the donkey.

Nathan's father was standing
talking with a few friends, waving
his arms about as usual.

Nathan grinned. His father's
hands were as busy as his tongue
when he talked!

Without a word the men were
untying Kidron from the wall.

Nathan sprinted down the street
like a shooting star.

How dare they take his donkey!

As he skidded to a halt he heard
his father ask:

'Why are you untying that colt?'

'The Lord has need of him,'
they said.

Nathan's father started to smile.

Then he winked in a secret kind of
way at his puzzled son, as Kidron
was led away.

Out came Nathan's mother carrying
Martha. She was smiling, too.

'Come on, Nathan,' she said.
'Kidron has a special job to do
today.'

The whole family trooped after
their donkey down the street,
where a large crowd had gathered.

'Look!' shouted Nathan, suddenly.
'It's my friend Jesus!', and he
raced on ahead to say hello.

Jesus came to Bethany quite often,
and Nathan loved him coming.

He always had a little something
for Tabitha and Kidron, and he
always made you feel special.

'Hello, Nathan,' said Jesus.

Jesus' friends were laying their
coats on Kidron's back, and then
Jesus climbed on.

A great shout of joy went up from the crowd.

'Hosanna! Hosanna! God bless our king, Jesus!'

Nathan was so excited. He picked up a branch from one of the nearby trees and waved it like a flag.

Lots of others did the same.

'Hurray for Jesus, the Lord!'

'Hosanna!'

More and more people crowded
the steep track, throwing their
coats down on the ground for the
donkey to walk on.

Winding all the way down the hill
and across to the lovely city of
Jerusalem they went, cheering
and singing, waving and dancing.

And Kidron's ears twitched and
his head nodded step by step,
as he carried Jesus, the king, on
his way.

Note for parents:
This story can be found
in the Gospel of Luke,
chapter 19, verses 29-40.